8 Steps to Amazing Webinars

Increase qualified leads, generate industry buzz, and drive people to your brand

Sharon Burton

Society for Technical Communication
STC IMPRINT
www.stc.org

8 Steps to Amazing Webinars

Graphics Credits

Cover Design: Bonni Graham Gonzalez

Disclaimer

The information in this book is provided on an "as is" basis, without warranty. While every effort has been taken by the author and XML Press in the preparation of this book, the author and XML Press shall have neither liability nor responsibility to any person or entity with respect to any loss or damages arising from the information contained in this book.

This book contains links to third-party web sites that are not under the control of the author or XML Press. The author and XML Press are not responsible for the content of any linked site. Inclusion of a link in this book does not imply that the author or XML Press endorses or accepts any responsibility for the content of that third-party site.

STC Imprint

The Society for Technical Communication Imprint highlights books that advance the theory and practice of technical communication. For more information about the Society, visit www.stc.org.

Trademarks

XML Press and the XML Press logo are trademarks of XML Press.

All terms mentioned in this book that are known to be trademarks or service marks have been capitalized as appropriate. Use of a term in this book should not be regarded as affecting the validity of any trademark or service mark.

XML Press
Laguna Hills, California
http://xmlpress.net

First Edition
ISBN: 978-1-937434-04-5

For David, who spends much of his marriage listening
to his wife talking to herself in her office

Table of Contents

Foreword v
1. What are webinars? 1
    Webinar benefits 2
    What you will learn in this book 3
    What you won't learn in this book 3
2. Why do you need webinars and who should run them? 5
    Don't jump on your horse and ride off in all directions 6
    Who should be running your webinar series? 8
    How much time is this going to take? 12
3. How do you choose topics? 15
    Audience audience audience 15
    Selecting the first few topics 17
    When to introduce other topics 18
    Scheduling topics 21
    Guest speakers 23
4. Which webinar technology should you use? 25
    Equipment 25
    Webinar software 28
5. How do you advertise your webinars? 31
    Writing the description 31
    Getting the word out 36
6. How do you get ready for your webinar? 43
    Put together your presentation 44
    Put together any polls you want to use 47
    Write the white paper or other giveaway 48
    Multiple presenters 49
    Assign a backup person 50
7. How do you manage the actual webinar? 53
    The week before your webinar 53
    Three hours before 55
    30 minutes before you start 57
    10 minutes before you start 58
    Show time 60

8. What do you do when the webinar is over? 63

    Manage the recording 63

    Review social media 65

    Use those leads 67

A. The top 10 mistakes in webinars 69

B. Useful information 73

    Suggested opening slides 73

    Example agreement with guest speakers 75

Index 83

Foreword

When I was younger, economists speculated that one day technology would eventually make the need for human labor obsolete. What would be left for us humans to do all day, when machines would eventually do all the work for us? As recent as the 1980's, there were only a few methods with which we could effectively reach our audience. Aside from door-to-door selling, sales professionals and marketers had limited options; the phone, the mail, the TV, the radio, or the newspaper.

As technology has evolved, quite the opposite of what those economists predicted has happened. We all seem to be busier than we have ever been. And, for marketers, the channels to reach our audience have exploded. The advancement of the Internet and mobile technology spurred the information exchange to explosive levels. Blogs, search, websites, online video, Twitter, Facebook, Wikis, Mobile applications, location based services, and the like have made the job of the marketer even more challenging.

How do we most effectively get our message to our targeted audience?

Webinars are one of those many choices our prospects and customers have to absorb more information. The time our audience invests in us and our webinar is a resource that's scarce. We better hit the mark when a prospect or customer decides to invest that time. As marketing and sales professionals, it's our responsibility to ensure not that we are moving the needle in terms of revenue to ourselves and/or employers and to ensure that the time that your potential audience invests has value. Otherwise, they'll never come back.

As Sharon points out in this book, when done right, webinars can be the most engaging and valuable method you have to effectively build that relationship, build your brand, and set your business up for success. Their reach is practically limitless, opening up the possibilities to a global audience that could not previously be messaged to as effectively.

Remember the movie Groundhog Day? In it, Phil (played by Bill Murray) wakes up each morning to discover that it's Groundhog Day again and again. He uses his experiences reliving each day to anticipate everything that could possibly happen, and in the end, is ready to run the perfect day, get the girl, and move on with his life. Similar to the movie, as you will read in the book, Sharon has done that work for us. She has used her experiences running countless webinars to anticipate everything for you, so you can run the perfect webinar and make a lasting, positive impact on your businesses.

She is a master at her craft, and when working with her, those very webinars helped greased the skids for my sales organization. Like you, we had a limited amount of "face" time with our potential prospects and customers. As a result of her perfectly executed webinars, we knew that when we invested the time to get face-to-face with those prospects, we were spending our time with better qualified opportunities. We were able to spend that "face" time focusing on their individual issues…and able to more quickly get to solution-oriented discussions.

With the tools in this book, you can succeed with your webinars…and you'll find that they will be easier and more rewarding than ever before.

Todd Caponi

About Todd

Todd Caponi is an expert in driving the revenue capacity of sales organizations both large and small. After owning and operating a sales training/consulting company, Todd has been Vice President of Worldwide Sales for two organizations, and is now responsible for global sales enablement with the leading technology company in the interactive marketing space. He also works as an executive coach and sales advisor for the NZTE (New Zealand Trade & Enterprise), advising New Zealand-based companies on their United States sales strategies.

Todd won the American Business Award "Stevie" in 2009 in the category of Worldwide Vice President of Sales of the Year, beating out other finalists including the Vice President of Sales of FedEx.

1

What are webinars?

In this step

- What are webinars?
- What you will learn in this book
- What you won't learn in this book

In the past, if you wanted to educate people about your product or service, you rented expensive hotel conference rooms, paid employees to travel, and fed attendees. Customers loved the seminar experience because they could ask questions, see and learn new things, and they got lunch. You could only attract people if they were in your local area and could be away from the office for the day. The per-attendee cost was very high, so only the larger companies could afford to do it.

But the world has changed. Now even small, one-person companies can afford to host and produce online seminars – called webinars – to educate people about available products or services. Now you can educate customers from any location with a high-speed internet connection. Your customers and potential customers can log in and watch your presentations, ask questions, see and learn new things – all while they eat their lunch or ride the train home. The per-attendee cost can sometimes be measured in pocket change.

Webinar benefits

With webinars, you can reach out to anyone in the world who is interested, regardless of time-zones. If you record your webinar and make it available for on-demand viewing, people can still see your content and learn at their convenience. No one has to travel.

Even more exciting, you can actually interact with customers and potential customers in a brand-new way. You can have a conversation with people interested in your products or services and find out what they want and need from you. This can significantly increase your responsiveness in both products or services because your customers are telling you directly what they want to purchase.

Webinars have additional benefits as well. You can use them as a way to capture information from an internal expert about process and best practices and share that with employees and customers. Many companies have people who are experts in important areas. If these people leave the company, that knowledge goes with them. Webinars can be used as a way to capture some of that knowledge and preserve it.

Finally, every company I know wants more sales leads. Most companies try advertising in industry magazines or place advertisements on websites. These typically don't get the response you hope for and are very expensive ways to attract leads. Webinars can be a great way to attract leads from people who are inherently interested in your topics, which are related to your business.

Not all webinars series are created equal. A bad webinar topic, a badly run webinar, or an incoherent series makes you and your company look clueless. In this book, I'll show you how to set up and run a successful webinar series, one that enhances your brand, attracts customers, and generates leads.

What you will learn in this book

Each chapter in this book is a step on the way to creating amazing webinars that your customers will come back to time and again. I've run hundreds of webinars over the past few years and attended at least as many. A poorly run webinar is a waste of everyone's time, which frustrates the attendees and makes the company look out of touch. A well-run webinar is an enjoyable experience that makes the attendee want to come back for more. But a well-run webinar doesn't happen accidentally.

I'll show you how to select the right person to run the webinars and select the right webinar topics for your company. We'll look at how to promote your webinars to get the most attendees possible, and which webinar hosting product is right for you. You'll learn how to get ready for a webinar, what to do during it, and what you need to do after it is over. In Appendix B, you'll find some introduction slides I use to help frame the webinar. I've also included an agreement I use when I have guest speakers.

You'll learn how to create a professional webinar series that makes you and your company look good. In this economy, that's a competitive advantage you can't afford to miss. If your time is short – perhaps you're hosting a webinar tomorrow – Appendix A has a list of the Top 10 mistakes people make. You'll want to review that right now. Before it's too late.

What you won't learn in this book

I'm not going to tell you how to create useful slides in PowerPoint or how to conduct an effective product demonstration. Nor am I covering how to use the various social media outlets. I'm assuming you know how to do these things – if you don't, you can use Google to find more information. These are good skills to have and will help you better create and manage your webinar series. If you are uncertain about your skills in these areas, spend an hour or so reading about them, using Google as your guide.

I'm also not going to tell you what specific topics are best for your company. I have no way of knowing that because I don't know the industry you're in, what your competitors are doing, and what the new things are in your field. I'll show you ways to find out this information, but you have to use your knowledge of your field to decide what your audience wants and needs.

2

Why do you need webinars and who should run them?

In this step

- What's the goal of your webinar series?
- Who should run them?
- How much time will this take?

There are several reasons why you should be running a webinar series. One or more of the following (listed in no particular order) may apply to your specific company:

- Add value to your brand
- Generate industry buzz
- Introduce potential customers to your products
- Position your company as a leader in the field
- Present related secondary topics to interest possible customers
- Support current users with in-depth demonstrations on advanced topics

All of these result in different webinar topics in your series. That's OK – you should have a variety of topics pitched to different audiences in your series. More about that in Chapter 3.

But perhaps the main reason you should be running webinars is that your competition is doing it. And they're reaping all the benefits. By not running webinars, you are missing the chance to make you and your products or services shine. Your competitors are positioning themselves and their products as leaders in your field. That leaves you looking, well, not good.

Don't jump on your horse and ride off in all directions

Just because your competition is running webinars doesn't mean you should run right out and start doing it, too. You need to plan what you're doing to get the most impact out of your webinars. Ask yourself why you want to run a webinar series. What is the point for your company? What do you hope to get out of the effort? Do you want more leads? Do you want to position your company in a certain way, perhaps as a leader in topics related to your industry? Do you want to drive more traffic to your website?

Until you know why you want a webinar series, you don't have a way to measure success, except by sheer number of sign ups. The number of signups is not necessarily a bad way to measure success, but if these are not leads you can convert to sales, this may not financially be worth your while.

If you want to increase sales as a result of the webinar series, it's better to have 10 highly qualified people attend your webinars than 1,000 completely unqualified people. If you're trying to generate buzz about your products, then netting 1,000 people who may not buy your product but who will talk about the cool products they just saw is great.

For example, I ran a series of educational webinars for a company. Most of these were not about any of our products – the point was to position the company as the place to go for expert knowledge in the field. We offered webinars geared to everyone from beginners to experts in the field, covering everything from the practical to theory. In a year, based on word of mouth, the company was considered to be the most knowledgeable about the field as compared to the competition.

You may not see the results of your webinar series until a year after you start. It can take time for the audience to grow and for your positioning to start working. You can't make decisions about the entire series until you've been at it for a year. At that point, you can make informed statements about what is working and what isn't and how close you are to meeting your goals for running the series in the first place.

This is not to say you shouldn't evaluate the webinar series and the topics on a monthly basis. Regularly evaluating topics and attendance helps you to discover what is resonating with your audience. Knowing what your audience is interested in allows you to do more around that area of interest. Knowing that few people attend certain topics tells you that you either pitched the topic poorly or your audience is genuinely not interested in that topic. This allows you to make course corrections.

Spend some time deciding why you want a webinar series and what the results are for your specific company before you start planning it out. What's the goal? Is it okay if it takes a year to reach that goal? What would be the goal after that? Do you want a goal after that?

Who should be running your webinar series?

After you decide why you want a webinar series, you need to decide: Who is responsible for the series and its content? This is one of those seemingly easy questions that can quickly become a nightmare corporate turf fight. Clearly, someone or some group in your company needs to be responsible for the webinar series so it has cohesion and an apparent plan to attract people. Several groups may seem like naturals.

Marketing

Marketing wants to run the webinar series because getting the word out about your products or services is what marketing does. So, clearly the webinar series should be run from marketing.

This can be a great idea, if your marketing group talks to other groups and includes them. If your marketing group is savvy about your customers and what they want and need, this can be a great solution.

If your marketing group is very good at creating slick ads and tracking click-thru rates, then having them run the webinar series may be a recipe for disaster. A webinar series that's all about shiny and not about value to the attendees is not going to go well. Word will get out that there is no content and attendee rates will drop off quickly.

Sales

Sales wants to run the webinar series because it's selling product to customers and that's what sales does. So, clearly the series should be run from sales.

This can be a great idea, if your sales team understands the products or services deeply and understands the customers and their problems at a deep level. Most organizations don't have a sales team like this because really good sales people are skilled at selling, not understanding the customers and their issues at a deep level.

If your sales team is driven by the sales numbers for this month, having them run the webinar series may be a very bad idea. Webinars full of "selling" are usually a failure. People won't sign up to be sold – it's not that interesting. Word quickly gets out that the webinars are nothing but a sales pitch and attendee rates will drop off, if it ever picked up in the first place.

Customer support

Support wants to run the webinar series because it's supporting products and that's what support does. So, clearly the webinar series should be run from support.

This is generally a bad idea all the way. Support reps are interested in one thing: reducing support calls. They want to run a webinar series that prevents people from calling. So they typically wind up running a webinar series of solutions to product problems. Sales and marketing have a fit because it looks like the products are full of problems, and if you look at the upcoming webinars roster, it's hard to argue with that perception.

Training

Training wants to run the webinar series because it's teaching people about the products and that's what training does. Training may already be using long-distance training tools, making webinars an extension of what training is already doing. So, clearly the webinar series should be run from training.

If your company charges for training, this can be an even worse idea. After all, you charge customers to learn to use your products. It's a revenue stream and no one wants to negatively impact a revenue stream. So you get a webinar series that's the introduction material from the training group, scheduled over and over. Since most people quickly move from beginners, you don't get the attendees you were hoping for.

Upper management

Upper management wants to run the webinar series because it's representing the products to the public and that's what upper management does. So, clearly the webinar series should be run from upper management.

If your upper management is closely connected to the clients and what they need, then this can be a good idea. If you have a small company, allowing your upper management to interact with customers and potential customers can be a real boost to your brand. It can make your company look like it cares at all levels.

However, if your upper management normally talks to other upper management and is not closely connected to what your customers want, this can go terribly wrong. Your upper managers can wind up talking as though they are presenting the annual report to shareholders, which will completely miss the mark for attendees. Upper management can actually chase away attendee signup.

I've seen a CEO, who considers himself a technology visionary, present a webinar on a new release of a product and spend 30 minutes on the "exciting new technology" the product is built around before he ever got to the product. If members of the news media were present, they stopped watching after 15 minutes because that's all the time they had to get the story. The webinar was a disaster, in that it didn't give the attendees what they were promised – a preview of the new product. And, because he's the CEO, it's hard to tell him gave a bad webinar. Try not to put yourself in that position.

If not these groups, then who?

The best situation is having all of these groups involved and signed off on a webinar series, but one person needs to be responsible for the series as a whole. Optimally, this person can give and manage webinars because they have the domain knowledge and can coordinate inside and outside your company to find guest speakers.

If you have a product evangelist in your company, he or she is perhaps in the best position to run the series. This person is already interacting with your customers, knows what the customers are interested in, knows the market and the competition, and is probably already the public face of the company. Product evangelists already stand across multiple departments in a company.

If you don't have a product evangelist now, then get one, even if it's informally. Often, you'll find you already have a great evangelist in your product management team if only you look. Make them responsible for the webinar series. They have the company and product domain knowledge to give several webinars themselves. They know your technology and they know your industry.

Another option that works for some companies is to hire a consultant to run the series. A consultant can come in with the experience you need and get the series up and going. At that point, you can train one of your staff or keep the consultant to run the webinars. A consultant can be a very reasonably priced option for a company that is understaffed and/or not willing to invest in hiring more headcount.

A mistake I've seen is to assign the series to the youngest (in experience) member of a group, perhaps in marketing. The reasoning is this new person has more time than the other, more experienced staff. This doesn't work out well, simply because the inexperienced person doesn't have the depth of business understanding yet to know how to run the webinars and probably doesn't have the domain knowledge to know interesting topics. They don't know why the company wants a webinar series, nor is it reasonable to expect an intern to effectively represent the interests of the company.

Regardless of who you appoint and what group they come from, they need access to all the groups I listed above. They need to pull topics and get speakers from all the groups to provide a full range of topics for the series. They need some experience in representing companies well to the public. Cooperation is one of the keys to creating an amazing webinar series.

How much time is this going to take?

After you assign a person to run the webinar series, you need to make sure he or she has the time to do it. Assigning a person who is already overwhelmed with tasks will result in failure. If you bring in a consultant, understanding how much time you will be asking from the consultant is important to understand if the consultant is reasonably priced. You have a better understanding of the services they should be providing.

Identifying topics, finding speakers, creating slides, promoting the webinars, running or presenting the webinars, and then performing the follow-up tasks can take 20 to 40 hours a week – or more if your series is successful, if your market is big or you have a lot of products.

It's important that you allocate the time to the person who runs the series. Don't take an already overwhelmed staff member and assign them the webinar series. And don't hire an intern for this project, either. Remember, the webinar series is representing your company and your brand to the public. You need someone who can do that and do it well. You don't want your company or your brands to look stupid in front of the very people you're trying to attract.

So what are the sort of tasks you can expect your staff or consultant to be doing to run an amazing webinar series?

You can expect at least these sorts of tasks:

- Research into what the competition is doing
- Watch social media and conferences for topic ideas from your industry
- Develop ideas for webinars
- Schedule webinars
- Find and manage guest speakers
- Write webinar content, including white papers
- Actually run the webinars
- Follow up with attendees

- Write survey questions and evaluate results
- Evaluate the topics for effectiveness and value to the audience
- Present webinar status reports at regular intervals
- Import the attendee list and, monthly, download the recording viewer lists

All these activities take time, and that time is well spent if you want to run an amazing webinar series. Not allocating the time will give you mediocre results and you won't understand why the webinar series isn't taking off the way you expected.

3

How do you choose topics?

In this step

- Who are you targeting?
- How do you select topics?
- How do you schedule topics?
- Should you use guest speakers?

Now that you understand why you are running a webinar series and you've assigned a person to run it, you need to decide the curriculum. This is one of the make-or-break areas in planning your webinar series. If you choose the wrong topics, no one will attend. If you choose the right topics, your series is going to take off.

Audience audience audience

The kind of webinars you give depends on who you want to attract. You may want:

- Current customers
- Potential customers
- Decision makers

- C-level executives
- Industry influencers
- And more

You probably can't address the interests of all these groups in the same webinar. Select one group you want to target. I strongly recommend going for the easiest audience first so you can gain experience in running your webinar series with a lower-stakes group. For example, if you target C-level people for your first webinar and it doesn't go well, then you've lost credibility with that audience for future webinars.

In general, current customers are going to be more forgiving if you are still working out the kinks. You have already engaged them enough that they purchased your product or service. They feel they have some relationship with you. People are always more forgiving if they feel a relationship.

That said, the forgiveness will only get you so far. If you don't deliver good content in your webinars, then even your current customers will be less than happy. They may spread the word that you don't quite know what you're doing. So it's important that you make sure your webinars contain good, useful content from the first one offered. If people leave feeling like they got useful information, then they will forgive issues.

Notice I'm talking a lot about feelings here. That's because a webinar series is a way to create or build on a relationship. In relationships, people get their feelings involved, sometimes over their logic. You know this already – you may purchase your wine from a local wine store, for example, where they know you and remember that you like dry reds. The wine costs a little more than at another store, but you feel good when you shop here because you have a relationship with the clerks in the store. That feeling of relationship is what we're trying to create in your webinars.

Selecting the first few topics

After you identify the audience you want to attract first, it's time to decide the first few webinar topics. The following is a list that I use to start planning:

- Advanced topics for existing customers
- Product demonstration
- In-depth product dives
- Results of a survey we just did on X
- Top 5 or 10 things you need to know about…
- Where the industry will be in a year

All of these can be great webinar streams overall. But because you can't do all of these topics at once, pick a topic that's appropriate for your selected audience. For example, if you decided your existing customers are your audience, then selecting a more advanced product feature that solves a common problem would be a great topic. Additionally, you probably already have the knowledge for this webinar in-house. This is a natural topic and should attract a lot of interest from your most friendly and engaged audience.

I like advanced features that solve customer problems as webinar topics a lot. While you probably won't get many new leads, it's a great way to show your engagement with your customer base, to show how your product solves pain, and to generate goodwill in your customer base. It's also a great way to hear from your engaged customers who are using your product to find out what they're thinking and doing. Customers feel you are interested in them, their problems, and their thoughts about your products or services. It's really a win on both sides. You are banking goodwill in your most engaged audience base.

Don't decide you're going to target existing customers and then do a product demonstration. This is a mistake because you're telling people who already use your product about what your product would be like if they used it. All that goodwill your existing customers have for you leaves in minutes (along with the attendees themselves) because it's insulting to your audience. You clearly didn't understand who you were talking to and what they needed. Getting these people to attend another webinar will be challenging because you insulted them the first time.

I saw a very large company do this once with a tool that has a large market share in their industry. They advertised the webinar as a chance to learn things you didn't know the product could do. I'm certain the attendance signups were off the charts, simply because of the market share. The first 20 minutes of the webinar (the length of time I stayed) explained the product and all the reasons why one would use it. Everyone on the webinar was probably already an expert in the product. We knew what the product did and why one would use it – we were all using it! Maybe the last 40 minutes showed things we didn't know the product did, but the people I know all left because we felt we were wasting our time. That webinar is still mentioned some five years later as an example of how out of touch with the user base that company is. With one webinar, they lost credibility regarding their own products.

When to introduce other topics

After you're confident in delivering webinars, you're ready to start adding other topics. Some of the best-attended webinars are the "Five things you need to know about…" The topic can be your tools or trends in your industry. If you want to attract decision makers and C-level people, pick five trends you see in your industry that will be important in the next year. People love webinars that are built around lists.

Many companies do webinars on this topic at the end of or start of the new calendar year. Scheduling your webinar at this time ensures your webinar gets lost in the noise. A better time is to schedule your webinar at the beginning of a quarter or fiscal year, provided everyone in your industry uses the same fiscal year. It's going to make your webinar stand out and will increase attendance. Everyone wants to know what's coming and what they need to be preparing for in the short term.

If you are releasing a new version of an existing product or introducing a new product, then you have a great and compelling webinar topic. If advertised properly, you can not only get your existing customers to attend but also the media. We'll cover ways to get the word out about your webinar series in the next chapter.

I like to run webinar topics as a multi-threaded stream. Always run a stream that's product- or service-specific. These include:

- Product demonstrations for potential users
- New product releases
- New service available
- Deep dives into two or three tightly related features/services that nicely solve customer problems
- The five top reasons why people call support

Then I like to run a stream that's geared more to theory or trends in the field. These can include:

- Guest speakers in the your field, typically offering expert opinions
- Topics that are of interest to your customers but are not product-specific
- Top five coming trends you want to know about
- The results of a recent survey

Depending on your market, I like to add a tools-neutral educational stream. These topics can include intermediate to advanced general topics in your field. Think of these as a way to teach attendees about important topics in your field that are completely unrelated to your product but help people who are working in your field. You never mention your products.

For example, if you are a camera manufacturer, running a series of webinars around getting good candid shots when doing portraiture is a great idea. Regardless of the cameras the attendees are using, they will learn how to take better pictures of people, such as their children. Never mention your cameras in the entire webinar. This positions your company as the experts in photography, not just in making cameras. You're selling photography (and pictures of adorable children), not cameras.

The educational stream can be a hard one to sell internally. Don't be surprised if you get push-back that educational webinars need to be about your products. But this would be limiting your audience to only the people currently using your products. You want a broader audience – you want to talk to all people who are interested in photography, regardless of the camera they are currently using. After all, one day, they'll want to buy a new camera. If that potential customer thinks your company understands photography better than the other companies, your cameras must also be better, right?

When the economy collapsed in late 2008, I was working for a company that made business content authoring and publishing tools. Watching the daily massive layoffs, I realized there would be a lot of people needing to suddenly update their skills but who might not have the financial resources to do so. Free educational webinars was a great way to do that. I started a stream of webinars that covered intermediate to expert topics, pitched as vendor-neutral.

Initially, of course, there was skepticism that a vendor would be running neutral webinars. I kept my word and wouldn't talk about our products during the webinar, even when asked directly. Word quickly got out that this free resource was helping people update and refresh their skills. And of course, when these people found jobs, they remembered that we helped them through the scary, unemployed time. Needless to say, these webinars were money in the bank and bought huge industry goodwill.

Scheduling topics

How often should you be offering a webinar? As often as needed, which seems like I'm ducking the question. I'm really not. It depends on who you are and what you're doing.

If you are a small company with a few products or services, then running a webinar every week may be just right for you. With at least two streams in your series, you can run a product-specific topic the first and third weeks of the month, with another stream the other weeks. That means you have something interesting going every week and, hopefully, people are attending at least one time every month.

If you have more products or services, you may want to offer product-specific webinars more often. For example, if you offer 20 or more products, then you may want to offer a different product-specific webinar multiple times a week, every week, rotating the products through the offering. Schedule your theory and education topics in amongst the other topics.

For example, if you have a line of cameras, offer different camera-model webinars several days a week with a few general camera topics in there as well. Do the same thing with your cell phone line, etc. People who attend one of the theory topics may also attend a product-specific one, simply because it's a chance for them to learn more, especially if it's the same time tomorrow.

The important thing is to offer a mix of topics. You want to attract people who have all levels of interest in your products or your industry. Leads from either can be panned into gold, especially if they keep coming back for different topics. Clearly, the interest in the topics is there – all your sales team has to do is convert that into a sale.

The time of day you offer your webinar also depends on several factors. I like to schedule mornings because I'm a morning person and because I also think people prefer to attend webinars earlier in the day so they can still accomplish what they need to do that day. I've noticed live attendees for afternoon webinars are not as high as with the morning webinars.

If you are focusing on selling into the U.S., then 10 a.m. Pacific is a good time. It catches the West Coast but it's not too late for the East Coast. You can also nicely pick up most of Canada and Mexico at that time, too. If you want to pick up Europe and the U.S., then 9 a.m. Pacific is a better time. You catch the end of the day for most of Europe, as well as the work day for the U.S., Canada, and Mexico.

Regardless of the geographical location of the market you are targeting, find a time that covers the most people in that area. Understand, too, the world is global and you are going to get signups from people on the other side of the world. They may not attend live but they will want to see the recording. This is a good thing. If you consistently get a lot of signups from one geographical location, you might want to consider doing a special webinar just for that time zone.

I live in the Pacific time zone, but every now and then I'll do a webinar on a topic popular in India, which is 12.5 hours off from me. It's worth my time to schedule something special for this audience, even if it means I'm doing a webinar at 10 p.m. my time, when I'm normally happily sleeping. It builds goodwill with that audience and they appreciate the extra effort to adjust to their time zone. I've also done webinars for the Middle East at my 5 a.m. because it worked for the attendees.

Choosing the day of the week is one of the easiest decisions: pick Tuesday through Thursday. Mondays are tough because everyone is typically trying to get the week organized, and Fridays are hard because people want to finish their work and go home. Tuesdays through Thursdays are easier for people to schedule and attend. And because you are offering something you want people to find easy to attend, you need to schedule for their convenience, not yours.

Guest speakers

After your webinar series is stable, you may want to add guest speakers to the lineup. Guest speakers can add serious value to your webinar series. Guest speakers can also bring additional audience members who already know the speakers and always want to hear them. Guest speakers can also add credibility to your company, products, and webinar series because they are, hopefully, already known in their field. The shine rubs off on you.

You can use existing customers as guest speakers, especially if they have solved a particularly interesting or common problem using your products or services. If they streamlined a process, reduced a cost, increased time to market, or in any other way improved their business workflow with your products or services, then this sort of webinar is very popular because other people can learn from these Best Practices topics.

While you gain so much from working with a guest speaker, what do they gain from working with you? Why would they want to participate in your webinar series? Because it will probably bring them more business. Most of the guest speakers you'll want to use are expert consultants in their field. Consultants are always looking to expand their client base. Speaking at your webinar series helps them do that. If you're using existing customers as guest speakers, then this is a chance for them to show to the world how smart they are and to attract some buzz for themselves.

So how do you find these experts? Hopefully you know your industry or your customer base well enough to be able to think of several people you would like to talk. If you don't, then it's time to start watching social media, industry blogs, and conference topics, and to talk with your sales team.

It's out of this book's scope to explain how to use social media like Twitter to your advantage. But you should certainly find out how to use Twitter and Google keyword searches and how to follow influential people on Twitter. When we start talking about advertising your webinar series, this is going to be helpful information for you. You should also be finding blogs that are related to your industry and reading both the posts and the comments. LinkedIn also has groups based on interests that you should be following for industry news. Most conferences list the topics and speakers for the year and often the previous year. Who is presenting topics that would be related somehow to your product or service? These all inform you what people are interested in and who seems to know what. You need this information. This is where you find industry guest speakers.

Don't overlook your customer base – nothing sells for you like a happy customer. Talk to your sales team – they probably know a customer or two who are really happy and are using your products or service to solve interesting problems. Contact these people and see if they would like to do a webinar with your company. Perhaps entice them with some free product or service. If your sales team isn't helpful, talk to the marketing department – do they have case studies from customers? Can you contact them?

The point is to work with the other groups in your company to find these happy customers. Put together a Best Practices or Lessons Learned or some sort of useful, full-of tips webinar that people will want to attend. People love to learn how to do things better or solve common challenges.

In Appendix B, I include a webinar agreement I like to use with guest speakers so that everyone knows what the expectations are and who does what when. You should have something like this in place, making sure you've run it by legal counsel first.

If you want to record the webinar for future viewing, make sure that is written in the agreement, stating clearly who owns what. You shouldn't own the content of the webinar because it's not your content. Your guest speakers are helping you, so don't be greedy with their content. You want them back in the future. And make sure your guest speakers have a link to the eventual recording, too, for their marketing purposes.

4

Which webinar technology should you use?

In this step

- What equipment do you need?
- What webinar software should you use?

To run a professional webinar series, you need the right equipment and software. The equipment is easy to get and doesn't need to be expensive. Webinar software is free to reasonably priced. If you have a computer and a high-speed internet connection, you can start your webinar series for less than U.S. $50.

Equipment

To run a professional webinar, you need:

- A decent computer
- High speed Internet connection
- A headset/microphone or a phone
- (Optional) a web camera

Computer

Any business-level computer will work for broadcasting a webinar. You may need to turn off everything else to get all the processor speed available, but you want to do that anyway to prevent accidentally broadcasting your email notices or having a Skype conversation request broadcast during your webinar. Obviously, the faster the computer, the happier you will be and the faster the recording will render after the webinar is over.

Internet connection

Your Internet connection needs to be stable and at least DSL/cable modem speeds. Because you are probably shoving data and VoIP through the connection, speed is important. That said, most webinar software allows you to call in for voice, typically at long-distance rates. I was once part of a multi-speaker webinar in which one of the speakers was traveling in Eastern Europe. He connected to the webinar using essentially dial-up speeds and called an international phone number for the voice. While it was fragile and he was mindful of slow screen refreshes, it did work.

Microphone and speakers

I prefer to use a headset/microphone attached to my computer instead of a phone if possible. It leaves my hands free to work the computer during the webinar. The sound quality is better for the attendees and I can more clearly hear my backup person if needed. I also dislike trying to clutch a phone headset to my head and working the webinar with one hand. While you can purchase hands-free headsets for most business phones, they tend to be expensive and don't always give you the sound quality you want. Bluetooth headsets, either with your mobile phone or your office phone, can sound echo-ey and not give you the sound quality your attendees need. Logitech makes good headset/microphones for under U.S. $50, and I've had good experiences with them.

If you are doing webinars where it would be helpful for people to see you live, consider a webcam. If, for example, you own a yarn shop, you might want to do a webinar series on knitting techniques. In this case, a webcam would almost be required, as so much of the topic is visual. It can turn a standard slide/voice presentation into something more personal by visually broadcasting you while you demonstrate.

If you are going to use a webcam, make sure you identify a presentation location with a pleasant background. If your office looks like mine, some clean up may be in order. The area behind you should be free from visual distractions, including bookshelves. You would be surprised at how many people are trying to read the titles of your books while you're broadcasting.

Don't use the speakers in your computer and purchase a stand-alone microphone or use the microphone built into your webcam. Neither of these are good audio choices. Using your computer to hear others results in sound from your speakers being broadcast into your stand-alone microphone/webcam microphone, which then broadcasts through your computer speakers, which broadcasts by the microphone, creating a strange audio rebroadcast that rebroadcasts. Very quickly, the audio becomes unbearable for you and your attendees. I strongly recommend the headset/microphone combination. You can hear and you can be heard, but the two are separate.

Tablets and other mobile devices

With tablets increasing in popularity, you may be able to present a webinar on a tablet. You'll want to test to make sure the sound quality on your tablet is what you need to give your attendees the best experience. If your tablet has a USB port, then you should be able to use a headset/microphone. If your tablet doesn't have a USB port, I wouldn't try a webinar on it for the same audio issues described above. Additionally, you may not be able to use your webinar software on your tablet as it might not be supported, especially if the software is Flash®- or Java®-based.

Your attendees may be able to attend your webinar on their mobile device, however, and this is a real plus. I recently attended a webinar using my iPhone and was delighted. I was traveling and couldn't be near my computer at the time of the live broadcast, but I was able to easily use my iPhone to connect to and attend it. Offering this option to attendees makes it easier for people to attend while in transit.

Webinar software

Which software you choose depends on your budget, total number of webinars a month, and the number of attendees you think you will have. These are factors you need to consider carefully as you start the software selection process. It may be that your company already uses GoToMeeting or WebEx, in which case the decision has been made for you. Ask the administrator to add you to the pool of users and you're good to go.

But if your company doesn't already have webinar software or your existing license doesn't allow for enough attendees, you may need to examine the options. This section provides an overview of the major options at several price levels. For specific details about the products and exactly what they will cost for your situation, contact the vendor.

When you start your webinar series, you may want to go with the plan you can afford (perhaps free) to see if a webinar series is interesting to your industry and how many people will attend. In many companies, it's easier to get permission to do a webinar series if the only direct cost is your time. But if the webinar series takes off, you'll need to start using a service that better meets your needs. More expensive does not always mean better.

Table 4.1 – Webinar services

Product	Total attend	Cost per year	VoIP
Adobe Connect	25	$600	Y
Anymeeting	200	Free with ads	Y
Click Webinar	50-1000	$350 to $2,400	Y
GoToMeeting	10	$600	Y
GoToWebinar	100-1000	$950 to $5,000	Y
LiveMeeting	25	$600	
ReadyTalk	25-2000	$500 to $1,000	Y
WebEx	8-25	$450 to $500	

As you can see, most of the webinar software vendors are priced in a similar range. Most have similar features for running webinars. When you start to research the vendors you are interested in using, ask if they charge additionally for each attendee or for VoIP, as this is where any additional costs are usually found. Ask what deals they can make for you if you purchase a year's worth of service at one time. Most of the vendors provide a good to serious discount if you purchase a year at once.

After you get the information you want, download the trial version and start working with it. Ask yourself:

- Is the interface easy for you to understand?
- It is complicated to create webinars? Can you create templates to reuse?
- Can you have multiple speakers without adding accounts?
- Can you create and send email notifications to people about webinars?
- Does it manage the signup process for you?
- Does it record? Is the recording in a custom format?

- Can you mute attendees?
- Does it host recordings? What's the space limit?
- Can you run polls during the webinar?
- Can you send surveys after the webinar is over?
- Does it provide reports on when people signed up and who attended?
- Can you brand the invitations, signup pages and other public-facing areas with your company logo and colors?
- Can you easily download signup lists?
- Does it require Flash® or other technology your users might not have?
- Can attendees chat with you and with other attendees?

These features are all available in the robust webinar software platforms and can really add to the experience for your attendees. They can also make it easier for you to manage your webinar series in a professional and simple workflow.

When you are comfortable with the pricing and the features, use the trial for a real webinar. Evaluate how it went and how well you liked it. If it worked well for you, you may have found your winner.

5

How do you advertise your webinars?

In this step

- How do you write the description?
- How do you get the word out?
- What's a good schedule for posting?

Now that you have a series planned and the tools chosen, it's time to write the overview and advertise the webinars.

Writing the description

The overview needs to clearly state the topic, who should attend, and three things the attendees can expect to learn. People are very busy and won't sign up for your webinar if the topic looks only vaguely interesting. They want to know concretely what they will learn so they can make the decision to take an hour out of their day to attend.

Notice this is all based on your attendees needs, not your needs. Stand in your attendees' shoes and ask yourself what you would want to get out of this webinar. "Learn about our new localization product" is not compelling to your attendees. They see no reason why they might benefit from learning about your product. "Reduce your translation costs by as much as 80%", however, speaks to them. If they're translating content and products, they're looking at a large translation budget and probably want to reduce that somehow. You've identified a problem they have and a way to solve it.

Write simply and clearly

I strongly prefer avoiding marketing speak in my webinar overview descriptions. I think the marketing words add noise and detract from the powerful message I'm trying to communicate. If marketing wants this:

> In this fast and exciting interactive hour, you'll see the industry's newest technology leveraged to reduce your localizations costs.

I prefer to rewrite it into something like this:

> During this hour-long webinar, see how you can save you up to 80% of your localization costs.

I want simple and direct words that communicate clearly to the attendee. People are busy, and if they can't understand the write-up, they won't sign up. Making them think and decode the language puts a burden on your attendees that's simply not fair. You're really saying "We couldn't be bothered to simply say what we're doing, so we wrapped it in all this silly language. But you should come anyway." Your signups will be far less than you thought they should be.

I also like to put numbers in when I can. An 80% reduction in localization costs is huge. It's an exciting thing for a company to think there may be a better way at half the cost. It's inherently interesting to your audience. But don't promise 80% if it's really 40%, thinking people will be happy with that number Because it is, after all, less than they're spending now, right? No. If you say they can reduce that cost by 80%, they want to know how that might work. It may not be possible for them specifically (due to safety requirements, for example) but they need to have faith in the numbers you're stating.

Provide the reason to attend

People also like to know what they can get out of the webinar. Listing three things they would learn by attending gives people a choice. If they already know one of those things, they see the other two and decide those would be nice to learn as well. You're asking for at least an hour out of an already overscheduled day – let people know up front what they can expect to learn.

There is another advantage to using simple and direct words: search engines. In my example rewrite above, the name of the product and the keyword "localization" are going to get picked up by the search engines. This is a good thing, as it makes it a little bit easier for your content to rank higher on web searches. Over time, the search engines will rank you higher and higher, as you reuse those keywords and other related words. Don't forget to use those words in the title of your webinar as well.

Make sure your write-up is short – I don't go much over 150 words and try to use bullets. I want the write- up to be scannable and have the key points visually stand out so people can quickly see why they might want to attend. Resist the temptation to put everything you ever thought of for this webinar in the write-up. And use the standard inverted structure format – put the most important information in the first sentence, as I do in my example below. Then let the next two sentences amplify that sentence and include, perhaps, who should attend. Add the three points attendees can expect to learn. Finish by identifying the audience that would benefit from this webinar.

Sample write-up

Here's an example of an effective write-up:

> **Reducing your localization costs – 9 a.m. PST, June 30, 2012**
>
> During this hour-long free webinar, see how you can save up to 80% in localization costs. Most companies must deliver information in multiple languages, but the cost can be enormous. A better workflow, the right tools, and standardizing your content can significantly reduce these costs. Learn:
>
> - How to improve your localization workflow overall
> - How Product XX streamlines the localization process
> - What standardized content is and the cost benefits it can bring you
>
> This webinar will provide valuable tips and best practices for people responsible for managing localization costs. To sign up for this webinar, go here: *[link to webinar signup page]*. We also record our webinars for future viewing. Click here to learn more.

This write-up is attendee-focused, in that it doesn't talk exclusively about the product. It's focused on the business benefits to the attendees by identifying a problem they face. We have three reasons for attending, so people can see at a glance what they'll learn and we identify the people who might be interested. The entire write-up is 110 words, so it's short and concise. People see the topic, the information they expect to get and who should attend. It ends with a call to action and an invitation to find out about the recordings available for on-demand viewing.

Now, go put that write-up in your webinar tool of choice. When you are done, you should get a signup link for you to share so people can sign up. Hang on to that link because you're going to use it a lot.

Most webinar products allow you to ask for more information from the signups than their email. If one of your goals for running a webinar series is to get more leads, your instinct is to ask everything you can think of to qualify the lead when they sign up. Don't do this. Really. I'm not kidding. Trying to fully qualify people at webinar signup makes the procedure hard and time-consuming. People browse away from things that are hard and time-consuming online. You want people to easily sign up, so ask for the least amount of information you need – name, email, and phone number, for example.

I know of a very large company that has one of the most painful webinar signup processes I've ever seen. To sign up, you go through this process:

1. Go to the page that lists the webinar you want to attend.
2. Log into their site with your existing login. Or create a new login, get a confirmation email, respond to the confirmation email and then log in.
3. Find the webinar, again, that you are interested in from a long list.
4. Provide:
   - your name
   - email
   - phone number
   - role in purchasing for your company
   - the total number of people in your company
   - your state
   - your country
5. Click Sign Up.
6. If there is another webinar you want to sign up for, repeat the entire process again.

I understand marketing's urge to want all this information, but all the information required for this signup process makes the process painful. I would have to be very interested in the topic to be willing to go through all this again, and I'd have to, because all this information is required each time. Why can't it get saved with my login so all I'd have to do is verify it the next time I try to sign up? Why make me provide the information each time as though they'd never gotten it from me before?

Let's not do this to your attendees. Ask for what you really need to follow up with people. It's more work on your end later, but it doesn't irritate people who just want to sign up for your webinar.

Getting the word out

After you your write-up is ready to go, it's time to get the word out. There are a lot of ways to do it, so I'll hit some highlights in this section. Most of these cost nothing but time, although that time could be considerable until you get the rhythm of it. Some of this can be automated with social media aggregate tools, such as HootSuite and Dlvr.it. Either talk to your social media person or look those tools up. They're both free, and pretty easy to learn, and contain some good advanced features that help automate certain tasks.

Your website

Obviously, you want a place in your website for people to see your webinar list. Create an entire section for Upcoming Webinars and Webinar Recordings. Think and plan ahead to when you'll have 30 recorded webinars available for people to view on demand. Make a visible link from your home page so that people can go directly to the webinar page. You want an easy and clear path to the webinar list.

I like to organize the upcoming webinar list in a table by date, from soonest to further in the future. I don't like to list more than a month in advance, but

I certainly want at least four weeks of webinars listed. You want the list to look like you're very busy with topics because interest is so high. Include the title of the webinar, that first descriptive sentence, the date and time, and a link to the signup page.

The recording page where you put the recordings of past webinars is tougher to organize well. I see a lot of companies organize by date, most recent to oldest, and that's certainly one way to list them. But if you are presenting multiple streams, perhaps organizing the list of recordings by stream – or at least providing a way for your users to sort by stream – is a better idea. That way, they can focus on the type of webinar topics they're interested in. Any way you can help users find the topic or topics they are interested in is going to result in more viewers. When you get 50 recorded webinars, asking your viewers to sort by date to find the one topic they are interested in results in people simply leaving your site in frustration.

Your company's blog is a great venue for promoting your webinars. You can include write-ups for the next few weeks, and then write up something about each webinar when it's over, linking to the recording. These get captured by search engines and add to your search rankings as well.

Direct emails

Your company should have an email list through which newsletters and other information are sent to your customer base. Prepare an email about the upcoming webinars to go out to this list, with direct links to the signup pages. I don't like to include the entire write-up in these emails, as I think it makes the email too long to scan. I put the name of the webinar, the date and time, and include the first sentence from the write-up. Create a link that says "To learn more and sign up, click here" so if the topic looks interesting, the reader has an easy way to find out more. It also makes the next four weeks of webinars easier for your readers to scan and find the one(s) they're interested in.

If your support group sends out emails, ask if you can include information on the next three or four webinars in them as well. Your sales team may also regularly send emails to customers, and details about the webinars should be included in those as an added value your company is offering. Leverage all the customer contact methods your company uses to spread the word.

Social Media

Social media is a fantastic way to interact with your users. If you are providing interesting webinar topics, your social media followers will spread the word for you. I'm not going to teach you to use social media or cover all possible options (there are plenty of books and blogs to help you with that), but I will give you some tips to make sure you're using social media effectively to get the word out.

seems to be the mother of all social media. Your company may have a Facebook page. If you have business-to-business products or services, you're not going to get much traction from advertising on your company Facebook page, although you should still post there. People look at Facebook as a place for their personal online life. They don't look for business solutions there. But if your products or services are consumer related, this can be a great place to post. If you are a cosmetics company, for example, and you want to do webinars about using cosmetics, Facebook can be a perfect place to post about your webinar series. Expect people to "like" and share your posts.

Google+ seems to be increasing as a social media site. Consider posting there, but be aware that you may not get much business-to-business traffic from it. As with Facebook, it seems to be more focused on personal life interactions. But if you're a consumer products or services company, you may get a lot of attention from Google+.

When you were looking around social media for topics your industry is interested in, you probably saw keywords, such as #techcomm. In these are called hash tags. Content can get picked up and republished by sites such as paper.li based on these hash tags. This can expand your tweets to an audience that might have missed your announcements. You want to use hash tags responsibly in your tweets about your webinars.

For example, you might tweet:

> Free webinar: Reducing your localization costs – June 30 2012
> 9am Pac #techcomm *[insert link to signup page here]*

As people search Twitter for information, they might search the hash tag #techcomm. If they do, they should see this tweet. Undoubtedly, someone has created a paper.li using the hash tag #techcomm (I did, as a matter of fact) and people subscribe to it, hoping to find valuable information they might otherwise have missed. Your content, with your link, should show up in that paper.

Ah, you may be thinking, "I see several words that are valid hash tags. Why don't we use them all in one tweet?" Because we are going to be tweeting and retweeting about this webinar about once a day for perhaps as long as three weeks. We need to vary the tweet because Twitter won't accept an identical tweet. We need to come up with variations about this webinar, and one of the ways we can vary is by hash tag. So the next time, we may decide to use #webinar and after that, we'll use #localization, and so on.

We want to post at least once a business day for at least two weeks about each webinar. Vary the words you use in each tweet. Remember that different time zones are getting your tweets at different times, so if you are interested in an international audience, consider tweeting at different business hours each day.

While you could sit up waiting for different times so you can live tweet, you really should be using a tool like HootSuite or Dlvr.it and schedule your tweets over the course of the advertising window for each webinar. It's easier to get things up all at once and then not worry about it. It also lets you see all your scheduled tweets so you can make sure they are unique. If it's appropriate to your audience, you can also schedule posts to Facebook, Reddit, Tumblr, and other social media sites from one product. Both HootSuite and Dlvr.it allow you to see what people are clicking and which social media site they are clicking from so you can hone your posts and make better decisions about which media yield the most signups.

Don't forget to create posts for after your webinar is over that includes the link to the recording. A lot of people sign up to get that link because scheduling conflicts prevented them from attending live. I like to create posts about existing webinars to remind people the topics are available on demand. I'll post about a specific recording perhaps once a week. Watch the signups for the on-demand webinars jump the day after you post about the on-demand webinars.

LinkedIn and other user groups

If your product or service is such that there are news groups on LinkedIn, Google, or Yahoo, you have other locations to post about your webinars. Make sure you check with the group owner about the proper way to advertise about them, as some groups don't allow any product-specific postings while others are more tolerant. Some groups want all posts that come from a product vendor or service provider to start with a statement like ***I work for company X***. Regardless of the list etiquette, you want to follow it. You potentially can catch thousands of possible webinar attendees with one posting and can look dumb to thousands more by not following the rules.

When you post, include the following: the name of the webinar, the date and time and the first sentence from the write-up. Include the three things people can expect to get out of attending the webinar and a link that says "To learn more and sign up, click here" with the link to the signup page. Don't embed it in HTML, as some people don't use HTML readers for lists and may not see the link. Go for the lowest common denominator in your post to you get the maximum exposure.

Don't just post and then not come back to the list. Be prepared to answer questions on the lists, such as what day the webinar will be held, whether it'll be recorded and what time the webinar broadcasts in a given time zone. It can get irritating, because you probably included all this in the original post (except, perhaps, the time zone) but people are busy and you want them to feel they can ask questions.

If an important list doesn't allow posts by vendors or service providers, you can get around it by asking a friend to post for you. For example, I have four friends who normally participate on a list that is important to my technical communication clients but doesn't allow vendor posts. I ask a different friend to post about the webinar as though it is something they saw themselves and thought it might be useful to the group. I don't do it with every webinar and I spread the posts around my friends, who are happy to oblige me. Don't be tempted to create an email account that you think would never be tracked back to you and pose as someone else. You're going to be found out and the backlash will be ugly, really ugly, and the web has a long memory.

Others

If you have a guest speaker, ask them to use their sources to also spread the word. They have different clients and social media channels than you do, so you're casting a wider net. If this speaker is a big deal in your industry, consider doing a joint press release to generate some buzz with the media.

If your company runs advertisements in trade publications or websites, consider asking for a small mention in the ads with a link to the webinars page on your website. Don't mention any specific webinar by name in the ad, just that you have a new free webinar program available.

Timeframe for posting about a webinar

You've put together the write-up and want to start scheduling posts about your upcoming webinars. What's a good posting schedule, regardless of the social media you choose?

Table 5.1 – Posting schedule

Timeframe	Social Media	Groups and lists
3 weeks before	2 times a week	1 time
2 weeks before	4 times a week	1 time
1 week before	every day	1 time
The day before	3 times	1 time
The day of	2 hours before	NA
After the webinar is complete	an hour later, mentioning how exciting/full/etc. the webinar was	NA
The day after the webinar	post link to the recording	1 time
The next 3 months, or until you see viewing drop off significantly	Once a week with the link	Once a week with the link

Stagger the posting times to pick up attention. Try early evening posts for social media, because people like to check social media outlets when they get home from work or after the children have gone to bed. If you have multiple webinars, stagger the posting times on the same day so you don't post a bunch of things in 20 minutes and go silent. The point is to spread a net as far as you can. Monitor clicks to see if specific times of day work better for your audience. Then focus your postings on that time for future webinars.

6

How do you get ready for your webinar?

In this step

- How should your slides be structured?
- Should you use polls?
- Should you use a free giveaway?
- Do you need backup?

You can do all the planning and tasks I've given you so far and then still look foolish by screwing up the information in this chapter and the next. This is the meat of your webinar series and it's important. It's the customer-facing stuff and it matters.

Too often, I see a potentially interesting topic fall apart during the webinar because the presenter thought s/he could "just talk" and that would be enough. He or she, maybe, put together one slide that appears the entire time and then talks through the topic. Upper management is particularly bad about giving webinars this way. I think they are used to people just loving the sound of their voice and they assume that everyone is hanging on their every word.

Unless you're Steve Jobs, the President of the United States, or Jane Goodall, this couldn't be further from the truth. Almost no one is that inherently interesting.

I think a lack of preparation is rude and shows disdain for your audience. It says you couldn't be bothered to take the time to support your attendees in learning what you said you were going to tell them. It also says your company thinks this is a fine way to treat current and perspective customers. Don't be rude. Show your attendees the same respect you would show them in person. Be prepared so the audience can see you are ready to go and take this hour of their day seriously. It would be as if you've invited people to your home for dinner and you serve them stew ladled directly on a dirty table with paper cups of dirty water in a room that wasn't picked up for guests.

Let's start with putting together your presentation.

Put together your presentation

Your attendees expect at least a few slides, even if you're doing a demonstration of a product. Presentation slides are a way to ground your attendees in what you're doing and that that you're starting. You may stay with the slides for the duration of the webinar or you may move to a software product or even a webcam, but start with slides for the introduction.

I'm not going to talk about good slide design here because there are lots of books and blogs that can help you. If you're not certain what makes good slide design or the rules about putting information on slides, do a Google search to learn more. Just remember to use the company branding on your slides.

Make the slides relevant to the information you are going to talk about at that moment. So, if you are going to introduce yourself (which I strongly recommend you do), have a slide that has the same information to show on the screen. It lets people who are not strong auditory learners use their reading skills to get the information. You're supporting multi-modal learning in your audience.

I know a CEO who prides himself on not having much, if any, content on his slides. "It doesn't tie me to any specific information and keeps the audience focused on me" he says. It also makes his presentations and webinars very hard to follow. If you get distracted for 30 seconds, you lose the thread of what he's saying and he's provided no way for you to fill the gap. He assumes he has your complete and total focus while he talks, which is simply unrealistic.

Opening slides

I start with a slide that has the name of the talk, my name and contact information, and a note about starting the webinar at three minutes past the hour. This sets the expectation for people as soon as they log in to the webinar about when it will start and the topic at hand. I copy that slide and remove the reference to the start time as my second slide. Because I almost always record my webinars, I'm going to start recording when I show the second side. Having my contact information on the slide helps people to know right away that I'm open to being contacted if they have any questions after the webinar is over. It makes me look approachable and available for further conversations. It humanizes me to the audience.

I briefly introduce myself at the start of the webinar so people know a little about me and my background. If I'm taking to other technical communication professionals, for example, I also talk about my particular biases if I know it's going to impact the information I want to talk about. I want to be relatable to the attendees. You may not want to cover your background, but you should certainly introduce yourself with your name and title and the company you work for. If you have a co-speaker, you should introduce them as well.

I always include a "Mechanics of How the Webinar Works" slide or two. Many people are very familiar with webinars, but it's still important to let everyone attending know how this works. I still get people who don't know they are muted automatically and get upset because they think I've "been ignoring me for five minutes!" if you tell people up front they're muted and that questions should be posted in the Questions area of the interface, you can stave off some of this potential upset.

Consider creating a Twitter hash tag for your presentation, especially if you think you'll have many attendees or you want to create buzz. For example, if you are showing a new release of a product or discussing the results of a recent survey, a hash tag lets your attendees develop some buzz for you. If you decide to use a hash tag, make it short but related to your webinar. For example, use an abbreviation for your company name or product, such as #WidgetV6.

At this point in the slides, I introduce either the topic or the guest speaker and get the meat of the webinar started.

Animations and questions

We all know that presentation software lets us have text and graphics fly around the screen in creative and unusual ways. We also know how annoying it is to sit through an in-person presentation that has no end of flying things. It's even worse in a webinar. You have no control over the bandwidth of your users. Flying animations suck up bandwidth, cause latency issues, and can result in crashing an attendee's experience. Or, your animation can get stuck on an attendee's screen in an unfortunate place and the screen won't completely refresh. All in all, it just results in a bad webinar experience for your attendee. Don't do it. Keep your slide design clean and simple.

If you use graphics, tables, charts, or other visual elements, make sure the type is quite legible on your screen. You're not projecting this content onto a large screen – odds are good your attendees are watching your webinar on a smaller screen than you're presenting on. Check to see if objects are visible at 75%. If not, redesign the slides. Don't forget to test your slides with someone using a smaller screen outside the office to make sure things are legible, too. Another set of eyes is always helpful.

While you may plan to answer questions as you go during the webinar, this is not always practical. If you have 250 live attendees, you simply cannot answer questions as you go through your material. I plan for about 10 minutes of questions at the end of the presentation. At the end of the webinar, I show a slide that says "Questions?" along with my contact information again. People often join webinars late and may not have seen my contact information previously, or the content of the webinar was interesting to them and they now wish to follow up at a later time. In any case, they have my contact information on the question slide, which I keep visible until we are either done with questions or the webinar is over.

I have example slides in Appendix B at the end of the book. Feel free to steal the structure and modify it for your own use.

Put together any polls you want to use

One of the ways to keep people engaged in your topic is to run several polls in the webinar as you go. It's a great way to get feedback from your attendees. I wouldn't ask more than three poll questions during the webinar, though, because it can detract from your topic. Most of the webinar software allows you to run polls. For example, we might want to ask the total number of languages people are localizing into.

As you write your presentation, think about places where you could ask the attendees a question. Think about what will happen if you don't get the results you expect. What if you think most people are localizing into 10 languages and this group of attendees are only localizing into one? If the rest of your presentation is built around making the business case for 10 languages, how will you spin this in real time during the presentation?

One way, using our example, is to find the industry standard when you put your presentation together and use that information on your slides and business case. That way, if the attendees are not localizing at that level, you can mention what the industry standard is and continue on without looking clueless about the topic and the responses, while informing people what the industry standard is. People like to know standards or trends.

Write the white paper or other giveaway

People love to get special stuff. At the end of the webinar, you should have a white paper or other document that will be available only to attendees. It doesn't have to be long or deeply detailed, but it should extend the topic you spoke of to a slightly deeper level. You can also use a Customer Success Story from marketing, if it relates to the topic. If you have a guest speaker, perhaps s/he has a more detailed white paper or article on this topic. You want something that people can share around the office to start more talk about the topic.

If you simply don't have a white paper or Success Story, or if such items aren't a good fit for your company and products or services, consider giving away a product or service, perhaps in a raffle that you'd hold live at the end of the webinar. Specify at the top of the webinar that you'll do this and that the winner must be present at the end to win. You'll make sure people are still with you at the end, and, depending on the product, you'll generate buzz for your next webinar. Don't use cheap trade show give-aways that cost you $2. People know cheap when they see it, and it will take away from the marketing buzz you're trying to generate.

Regardless of whether you're giving away a paper, product, or service, make sure you have that in place before you finish your slides.

Multiple presenters

Webinars with multiple speakers presenting the same topic can be a great format. You can share different opinions, discuss similar issues across industries, share a customer success story, or present different ways to think about a subject. These sorts of webinars can provide attendees with buckets of information they can use that very day. Multi-speaker webinars can also be a painful and awful experience for everyone.

If you have multiple speakers, assign one of them or yourself to be lead. One person must be the person in control. The lead is responsible for making sure everyone's slides are complete, that the slides are coherent, and for being in control of the technology. However, each speaker involved needs a complete set of the slides being used, and each needs to understand how the technology works, in case there is a problem.

For example, what happens if one of the speakers is suddenly hit with an Internet outage and is yanked offline? Can the other speaker take over and manage alone? What happens if, five minutes into the webinar, a fire alarm goes off and one speaker must leave his/her building? Can the remote speaker continue on until the other speaker rejoins? I've seen both of these situations happen and it is painful if there is no backup plan. Things happen beyond your control and you must have a plan for remaining professional and carrying on.

Having a backup plan means all the speakers understand the webinar technology and the topic well enough to manage by themselves if needed. Everyone has practiced to know how to handle things if one of you suddenly vanishes. Everyone knows what to do and can continue as gracefully as possible. Because this is going to happen to you at some point in your presenting life.

Trust me on this.

Assign a backup person

Assign a second person (or third, if two people are presenting) to join you for your webinar. This person has a functionally non-speaking role and will simply manage easy questions from the attendees and help anyone with technical issues. You cannot present and manage the technical issues of 14 people at the same time. I've tried it and it doesn't work. If you have a guest speaker, you can be the backup person for him or her. But someone has to be there to manage the people who can't get the audio to work, who can't find the call-in number, who don't see anything on the screen, and so on. Solving these issues typically takes three to four minutes per person and that's time you are not talking about your topic. Your attendees certainly don't want to listen to you do technical support – they came for your topic.

Because this person is going to answer the easy questions for you during the webinar in real time, make sure the backup person also knows something about your topic. It doesn't have to be in-depth, but s/he should know what you're going to talk about because they are going to get questions about what you're covering. If you are doing a webinar on a product, it's good if the backup person knows something about that product because they are going to be asked direct questions. You need to focus on your topic and providing the best webinar information you can. The backup person is supporting you.

Have this person walk through the webinar technology so that they understand where the Questions area is, what number, if any, should be called for the audio, or how the VoIP should work. Let them answer practice questions so they understand how the interface works. Discuss what "easy" questions they should answer and what kinds of questions you would like in the Questions part of the webinar. Walk them through your topic so they know what you're covering in this webinar.

It may be that you don't actually need your backup person often – perhaps everyone manages the technical issues easily and this particular group has only the kinds of questions you want to answer yourself. But that one time when half the group doesn't understand the technology and can't get things to work properly is when your backup person will be a life saver. Resist the temptation to fly alone because the previous webinar went so well. Always have a buddy.

I like to bring the backup person in verbally at the questions part of the webinar because s/he has been managing questions and knows what's getting asked a lot. I may not have been clear, or perhaps I assumed my audience knew something and it turns out they didn't. My backup person can rephrase several related questions into one more general question that I can then answer for the group. My preference is to give audio to my backup person and have a question-and-answer discussion with them. You may want to manage this in a different way, depending on your comfort levels and the presentation comfort levels of your backup person.

7

How do you manage the actual webinar?

In this step

- How do you prepare for your first webinar?
- What tasks do you need to do before the webinar?
- When do you need to do these tasks?

It's getting close to your webinar. You advertised, you created the presentation, you have the white paper or other give-away in place, and everyone knows their role on webinar day.

This chapter covers the tasks you need to do in the days running up to the webinar and the actual webinar. These tasks make sure the webinar experience for your attendees is professional and information-rich.

The week before your webinar

Watch the signups for your webinar to see if you are getting the attendance you're hoping for. You should see a spike in signups after every posting you make to your social media outlets and to lists. Use the analytics from HootSuite or Dlvr.it to see which outlets are providing you the most interest for your topic and where it's getting reposted. If you are new to webinars (perhaps this is your first), try not to be disappointed if the numbers are not what you wanted. It can take time to grow the series. Each attendee will hopefully tell others about the webinar. Word of mouth will help future attendance.

Make sure you send reminders to the people signed up a week before, the day before, and an hour before the webinar starts. People might lose the original email and the reminder is helpful. You may get people responding that they cannot attend, as something has come up. Personally respond to them that the webinar will be recorded and that they'll get a link to that recording the next day. This usually makes people very happy – after all, they were interested in the content of the webinar and they can still get the information.

Understand that 50% of your signups won't attend the live webinar. It can be very frustrating to have 100 people signed up and only 50 attend live. You can get discouraged about the topic until you recognize that this is normal – people signed up knowing they couldn't attend live but are counting on the recording. Make sure management has the expectation that a 50% live attendance rate is normal and expected and not an indicator of the overall value of the topic.

Test the technology

Regardless of single vs. multiple presenters and the webinar software technology you are using, you need to test the equipment and software with all presenters.

I recently attended a webinar with multiple presenters. The host's microphone was set to very loud but the guest speaker's microphone was set to very quiet. It felt like the audience was being yelled at and then whispered to as each person spoke. It was very hard to listen to the content. This could have been avoided had a sound check been done the day of the webinar.

Everyone who is going to be on the webinar needs to take part in the test. Don't assume all microphones will be set at appropriate levels, for example. You must test to make sure it provides your attendees with a good sound environment.

Three hours before

Your webinar starts in three hours and it's time to start preparing for the webinar. Use this section as a checklist of things to do to ensure everything goes as well as it can. If you're very confident about presentation, your webinar software, and the topic, you may not want to start this early, but if you are uncertain about any of these tasks, get ready three hours from start time. You have time to resolve issues without making yourself insane.

Regardless of how careful you were to state the time zone in the start time, you will get emails at least two hours before the start time asking why you haven't started the webinar yet. I have no idea why, in this global world, people can't figure time zones, but they can't. Additionally, people will send you last-minute regrets or ask if you will be covering a specific topic. Be near your email to help these people get sorted out. Be pleasant and upbeat and express your excitement in seeing them when it's start time. It's your first personal interaction with them and it matters.

About an hour before the webinar is ready to start, find a quiet location, such as an unused meeting room with a door that closes. If you have your own office, that's even better. Bring your laptop, your power cords, and a notebook to write yourself notes. If I'm doing a product demonstration, I like to have the main areas I'm going to be showing in order on a note card to make sure I know what I'm doing and in what order. If you do the same, make sure you have the note card with you.

Bring water – not soda – in a closed container, like a bottle, to lubricate your throat as you talk. The carbonation in soda can tighten your vocal cords, making the pitch of your voice higher, which is not good if you have a naturally higher pitched voice or are a little nervous. The closed container helps you avoid disaster if you knock it over on your laptop as you talk.

Reboot your computer. Most webinar software sucks up computing resources and you really need a fresh machine. If your computer automatically logs into a VPN, disconnect and close the software, if possible. Close Skype, your messenger software, and any other unneeded software. Any messages these programs can show to your desktop may also be broadcast to your webinar. For right now, keep your email open to answer any questions from your attendees.

Open and do a final walk-through of your presentation to remind yourself what you're talking about. If you are doing a product demonstration, open and get ready any software you will be showing. If I'm doing a product demonstration, I like to make sure that what I want to show is available and what I listed on my note card works properly.

A note about using virtual machines to show software products: Don't do it. Many companies have a robust version of their software product on a virtual machine for staff to use for client demonstrations and such. It is often very sensible to have a virtual machine to make sure the demonstration version of the product is showing the approved demonstration information.

But during a webinar, you have no control over the speed of the virtual machine or over the bandwidth issues of your audience. The lag time of the virtual machine can be multiplied by five times over the webinar broadcast. This makes your product look slow and unresponsive. If you explain you're working on a virtual machine and that there may be lag time, you look like you're using excuses to explain poor product performance. It simply doesn't work. And the one potential customer who is here to check the last boxes before they purchase is going to log in late, after your explanation of the lag time, and leave the demonstration horrified at the "performance issues". Nothing good comes from using a virtual machine to demonstrate software in a webinar.

30 minutes before you start

Thirty minutes before your webinar is scheduled to start, log in. All webinar software has a pre-broadcast mode of some sort. Use this mode to see if the technology is going to work and resolve any issues you may have.

- If you are using a webcam, it's time to make sure the webinar software can see it and that you're getting the results you're expecting.
- Make sure your VoIP headset and microphone is working or that your phone is functional and the phone number works.
- Test the volume of all the speakers' microphones.
- Test any polls to make sure they're still where you left them in the webinar software and that the questions still make sense.
- If you have a guest or co-speaker, make sure they are logged in and that all their equipment is working as expected.
- Make sure your backup person is online and can see and respond to test questions you pose.

I sound a little like a control freak here because, when it comes to customer-facing performances, I am. When it's time to start the webinar, I want any and all issues either resolved or identified so I can work around them. When I'm facing the public representing a company, I want to give my complete attention to the webinar and the experience of the attendees. Issues still happen, no matter how much testing and work you do, but the issues are fewer and more manageable if you do the preparation work.

I've attended webinars where the hosts clearly logged in three minutes before they went live. The result was that not everyone had a working microphone, or we watched the software being demonstrated slowly open while the presenter talked about what we were going to see if only the product would open. I've heard presenters be surprised by a slide and the content. This all looks so bad to the attendees.

It's fine to be fast on your feet and improvise in the moment, but it's very bad to look like the entire webinar caught the presenters completely by surprise. I think this shows a lack of respect to the attendees – you couldn't be bothered to make sure the mechanics worked before we started. And a company that can't be bothered to show customers and potential customers respect is not going to do well.

10 minutes before you start

It's time to shut down your email client and any non-webinar-related browsers on your computer. The only things that should be open are the applications needed for this webinar. It's time to start broadcasting your first Welcome slide. People will start logging in at least 10 minutes before to make sure their technology is working and that they're set to go. If you start broadcasting your slide, you give them a chance to work out any issues on their end, reducing the time your backup person needs to spend getting them ready to go.

Remember, after you start broadcasting, your attendees can hear you. They can hear any mobile phone conversation you may be having in the room or any chit-chat you and your co-presenters are having. Attendees can hear the comments of your backup person unless you mute him/her. I cannot stress this enough: Unless you mute yourself (and you will forget to mute yourself), everyone can hear everything happening around you. Now is not the time to make poorly thought-out jokes, say bad things about the competition, discuss a top-secret project, or, really, say anything you wouldn't want to see on the front page of the New York Times. You may not make the Gray Lady, but you will appear on Twitter. And it will go viral. Trust me on this.

At this point, make sure you mute all attendees, if the webinar software doesn't do that automatically for you. As people arrive, either you or your backup person needs to make sure that all attendees are muted. Do not depend on people muting themselves; for reasons I can't figure out, most people don't know how to do this with either their phone or their VoIP headset. Your attendees are in loud environments and you want everyone to hear you, not the noises in 250 environments.

When you get about five people, ask for a sound check. State that you are doing a sound check and ask people to type some phrase in the Questions area of the webinar interface. I like to use some phrase that relates to the topic of the webinar or simply ask them to type "Hello." After you are done with the sound check and have determined people can hear you, announce the webinar will start in XX minutes, and then mute yourself.

Start your webinar at three minutes after the hour. People are coming from other meetings or finishing up that email before they get logged in. Most of the technical issues that will happen with your attendees appear in the first five minutes after they connect. Starting three minutes after the official start time gives you and your backup person time to resolve these issues. Your first Welcome slide should state you will be starting at 3 minutes after the hour, assuming you are starting at the top of the hour. See Appendix B for an example.

At five minutes before and at two minutes before the official start time, unmute yourself and announce the start time. Thank people for coming, perhaps make some statement about your surprise at how many people are attending (even if there are very few), and then mute yourself again.

At the official start time, unmute yourself and start talking, perhaps about the weather or run a poll about the locations of your attendees. The point is to have attendees hear something going on when they call in at the official start time. You want them to feel you are on top of things and that this is all going to work out fine. I like to do a poll about the locations as it's a good warm-up technique – everyone is interested in where people are located.

Show time

At three minutes after, it's time to start. Switch your opening slide to the one without the three-minute warning on it and start the recording. From this point until you stop recording, everything you say and show will be in the final recording. You may do post-processing of the webinar, but assume everything will appear in the final version.

Always make sure you have a slide that states – and that you verbally state – the webinar is being recorded. Assure your attendees that none of their personal information will be disclosed in the final recording. In some countries, this warning is a legal requirement, but even where it's not, it's just polite. Let people know the recording will be available to them after the webinar is over if they wish to review it.

Thank people for giving you an hour out of their day and take the time to introduce yourself. If you can have a picture of yourself on the slide, so much the better. Unless you're using a webcam, you're just a voice coming through your attendees' machines. Let people have a face to attach to that voice. It makes them feel more comfortable with you.

Introduce your backup person and explain his or her function so it's not strange for them to see the name of someone else answering their questions. Remind attendees how to ask a question while you are talking and assure them there will be a question-and-answer section at the end of the webinar.

You want people to understand how to ask a question in this format and how it's going to get answered. Just because this is a technology-based presentation doesn't mean the people skills don't matter. I think they matter more in webinars because of the technology distance.

Now, start your presentation. If you have a guest speaker(s), introduce them and turn it over to them. Unless this is a discussion webinar, try not to interrupt the speaker unless you need to clarify for your audience. You invited this expert to talk – let him or her do that.

At the end of the presentation, in the final 10 minutes, the last slide has the word "Questions?" and your (or the presenter's) contact information. This is where you respond to the questions that kept coming up or that the backup person couldn't answer.

You have a decision to make here: Do you stop recording or not? I prefer to stop recording at this point and do the questions as non-recorded. I like to refer to people by their names when I'm answering their questions and I don't feel comfortable doing that when I'm recording. Additionally, I want added value for those who attended live and I think the question-and-answer period is an added value.

End the webinar on time. At the specified end time, thank people for attending. If the question-and-answer discussion is lively and you have the time, you can announce you can stay another 15 minutes but that if people need to go, you'll understand. If the question-and-answer period is winding down, you can end the webinar. Don't close down the webinar software until nearly everyone has logged out – sometimes people have one final but very important question.

When nearly everyone has left the webinar, close it down. Most webinar software will start rendering your recording when you exit the webinar. It's time for you to go for a short walk or get lunch, because this can take some time. I've had my computer take two hours to render the video. Working on your computer while it's rendering slows the process down further and can result in freezing the rendering completely. Just go for a walk, grab lunch, whatever you need to do for an hour or so while your computer renders the video.

What do you do when the webinar is over?

In this step

- What do you do with the recording?
- How do you review social media?
- What do you do with these leads?

While is a relief to finish a successful webinar, the work is not done. There are follow-up tasks to accomplish to maximize the impact of your webinar. This chapter explains how to get the most out of the recording and keep your customers and potential customers engaged.

Manage the recording

After you render your recording, you need to put it somewhere where the people who signed up can view it. Often, your webinar software vendor can host your recorded webinars for you. You simply follow the upload wizard and it's all managed. Most webinar software vendors also provide reports about who saw on-demand recordings when. Be aware that most vendors limit your space on their servers, so if you hit the space limit, you need to start deleting recordings. In my experience, most webinar recordings are 100 to 300 megabytes and they take up server space fast, especially if you have a successful webinar series.

If you decide to host the recordings on your site, then you will need to capture who sees it. These are additional leads that can add up over time if the topic is very popular or the speaker is well known. Most CRM programs will allow you to integrate a signup list with the CRM. This integration will take some programming time, at least, and may not be an option for you. You will also need to work with your webmaster to get the video on the website within 24 hours of the original webinar. In some organizations, this can also be difficult.

Do not put the entire recording on YouTube for the public to see because you miss potential leads. However, you may want to post excerpts of the recording to YouTube. This can be a fantastic way to generate interest in the webinar series and in a specific topic. If you have a person who is good at editing video – someone perhaps in marketing – you can work with them to pull enticing clips out of the recordings and get them posted. Don't forget to wrap the clips with company branding and a link to see the rest of the recording.

Regardless of who and where the recording is hosted, it needs to be made available within one business day of the webinar. Up to 50% of your signups couldn't attend live and want to see the recording. Making this secondary audience happy by being responsive to their needs shows you are responsive in general.

Most webinar software allows you to automatically send emails to attendees and no-shows at a specific time after the webinar is over. Use that feature to send emails with the link to the recording the next business day.

I prefer to have two emails:

- one to attendees, thanking them for attending, reminding them of one or two important points from the webinar, including the link to the recording, and linking to any white paper I promised
- one to non-attendees, thanking them for signing up, mentioning one or two key points from the webinar, including the link to the recording, and perhaps linking to any white paper promised

In both emails, I encourage them to share the link with other people who may be interested and to contact me with any questions. It's a personal touch and makes people feel special.

Most webinar software also allows you to create a survey that goes out all people who signed up. Use a survey to get feedback on the value of the webinar. I like to ask about other topics people would like to see. Some of my most popular webinars have come out of asking current attendees what else they would like to learn about.

Send the email with the recording link and the survey link out within one business day, again a week later and then three weeks after the webinar. People who didn't respond immediately often need time to digest the topic and perhaps apply the information before they want to respond.

Review social media

In a previous chapter, I covered reposting in social media channels about completed webinars and available recordings. This is especially important if people posted about your webinar while it was happening. You also should search social media sites for posts about your webinar. In the very connected world of social media, people often post key points from a webinar in real time, if they see truth or value in these points. You can learn what resonated for your audience by searching for these posts. I like to use these posts – with permission – on my webinar listings web page. It looks good and adds excitement to the future webinars. I also like to repost them over time, up to a week after the webinar, with a link to the recording.

In your search, you may find negative posts about your webinar, the speaker, the topic, your company. It's very tempting to respond to these posts but resist the urge, unless the post is factually inaccurate. If someone is stating an opinion, nothing good will come from you disputing their opinion and the whole thing will turn into a public flame war. Even if the comment is nasty and personal, do not respond. Often, this person posts nasty comments about everything because they are just a nasty person. You and your company will not benefit from interacting with them. Nasty is a sticky glue.

Instead, look at the posts and learn from them. Identify what topics people posted about to help you understand the marketing messages that resonated with your audience. Consider webinar topics that could be created from these messages. Examine the negative posts and decide if these are things you can improve upon – was your voice mentioned as dry or boring? If so, find a voice coach or practice to make your voice more interesting. Was an accent mentioned as difficult to understand? Did the speaker talk too fast? Was the topic too high- or low-level? Did the attendees want more examples? Fewer examples? These are all issues that can be fixed for future webinars.

If no one posted to social media, don't despair and decide this is all a waste of time. Sometimes no one posts, but that doesn't mean your attendees didn't get value. Look at the survey results to see how people rated the webinar and evaluate any comments they may have made. It's all a learning experience, and sometimes a webinar simply doesn't resonate with the audience the way you hoped.

Use those leads

Download the signups and get them into your CRM software. These leads need to be added to your email database so they can get future emails from your company. Additionally, it's good if your sales team can follow up with them, but this depends on your type of sales team. I've worked with inside sales teams that called every person from the list in their territory within a week to chat about the webinar topic and offer help. These sales teams leveraged the webinars as another way to continue the relationship sales method they used – to great success – with their customer base.

I've also worked with inside sales teams that were interested in the large accounts and didn't follow up with the webinar leads at all. They were too busy to follow up with each attendee in their region, even if the attendees were associated with an existing client. Personally, I think following up with at least the attendees linked with existing clients is a good idea. Often this customer is looking to solve a new problem, and there is a good opportunity for upselling that's been expressed by attending a webinar.

But it could be that you don't have an internal sales team because that's not the way your product or service is sold. These leads still need to be in your CRM so these people can get the marketing emails and emails you send out for future webinars.

The top 10 mistakes in webinars

This chapter is a quick list of the most common mistakes I see in webinars. Each mistake is discussed in detail in other places in this book.

1. Not advertising or providing enough lead time for word to get out

People want to attend your webinar. But giving them a week's notice or less that you're doing one is not enough time for many live attendees. Most people have very busy workdays and they need more time than that to adjust their calendars. You also need time for your social media outlets to get the word out further. The only time I allow less than two weeks lead time is if I'm doing a webinar announcing a new product release. If you don't give enough lead time, recognize that the live attendance rate may be a low as 30% because people are depending on the recording for on-demand viewing later.

2. Doing a bait-and-switch presentation

Don't publicize a webinar topic and then do whatever topic you want when the webinar starts. You asked people to give you an hour out of their day to hear a topic. They signed up expecting that topic. Don't change that topic because another topic is more interesting to you that day. Keep your promise to talk about what you said you were going to talk about. People want to trust you (and your company) to do what you said you were going to do.

3. Not being certain how the technology works

As an attendee, watching the speaker stumble though webinar technology is painful. It also casts doubt on everything that speaker is saying because attendees ask themselves, "How much can this person know if they don't know how to use the technology to present?" Attendees wind up dismissing the speaker and topic. Take the time to learn how to use the webinar technology. It's pretty straightforward and fairly simple. Multiple speakers talking over each other, not sure who is speaking for each part and not sure how to hand over control to each other is not a professional webinar experience. It's also rude because it looks as though you couldn't be bothered to prepare for a pleasant experience for your attendees.

4. Not starting or ending on time

The number of webinars I've attended where the speaker didn't start on time or went wildly over the stop time… Your attendees scheduled an hour out of their in-all-likelihood very busy day to listen to your topic. Show them the respect of starting on time. Have the "Welcome" slide up 10 minutes before the start time to welcome people to the webinar. End the webinar when you said you would. If the attendees wish to stay over with an extended question-and-answer period, that's fine, but finish talking about your topic when you said you would finish.

5. Boring voice and wordy slides

Not all of us have naturally lyrical voices with graceful and musical inflections. But you can learn to have a more interesting voice – broadcasters do it all the time. Because your voice is a big part of the webinar experience for your attendees, learn to make your voice interesting. A monotone voice sucks the excitement out of a presentation and leaves your audience depressed and sad. Record your voice to listen to how you talk, and, if needed, find a voice coach who can help. The investment is worth it.

Your slides should not have more than four to five bullets, total. If you think you need more than that, you're wrong. Go find a book or blog that talks about good information design on slides. If your attendees can't read the content, there was no point to you building the slide.

6. Not muting the audience

Most attendees are probably in their office or cubical when they attend your webinar. The typical business work area is a noisy place. People type emails, co-workers pop in to ask questions, other people have discussions in nearby cubicles. All webinar products allow you to mute the audience to reduce the noise distractions for the attendees. Use it. People came to hear what you have to say, not the clicking of keys on a keyboard.

7. Not using backup support

You simply cannot resolve the technical issues of 10 people and give your topic at the same time. Your attendees came to hear your topic, not listen to you resolve the issues of various people. You also cannot answer live questions from 250 people and present your topic at the same time. But you shouldn't ignore the questions that come in during the webinar. That's why you have the backup person – they manage these details while you focus on your topic.

8. Not providing a tip or related white paper or products

People feel they get value if they leave with a tip they can use that day or a white paper that explains something further or a Best Practice from other companies or a prize. This gives them something concrete to show for the hour they spent in the webinar. They can share whatever they get around the office, making them look smarter in their workplace. Winning products is always exciting because most people don't win much in their lives. Always provide that little extra value.

9. Not recording the webinar

Recording a webinar is not always in your control – the technology can crash, your speaker may decline to let you record (which is their right), or other challenges can present themselves. But it's important to record as many as you can. The world is global, and no matter what time you hold the live webinar, not everyone who wants to attend can make that time. Sudden meetings are called and people who thought they could make it can't. It's typical that up to 50% of your signups are expecting the recording to learn about the topic.

10. Not following up with attendees

Perhaps you have had a wildly successful webinar with more than 1,500 signups. You downloaded the information and imported it into your CRM software. Where it sits because no one is following up with these leads. These are people who are interested in a topic that relates to your products or services. Why wouldn't you follow up with them? Your company probably pays thousands of dollars to attend tradeshows, hoping to get half this many leads. You got them from one hour-long webinar at very little cost. Make sure that sales or someone is following up with all these leads, even if they are existing customers.

Useful information

This section contains slides and other things I find useful in running my webinars. They are included here to help you develop materials that are useful to you.

Suggested opening slides

These slides help to frame and set expectations for your webinars.

Webinar Mechanics
How does this work?

Who am I and why am I speaking?

- I'm Sharon Burton
- Content strategist and social media expert
- Eeen in the Tech Comm industry for nearly 20 years
  - STC Associate Fellow
  - Teach for:
    - STC Webinar Certificate series
    - Technical Communication to Engineering students at the University of California, Riverside (UCR)
    - Tech Communication certificate program at UCR Extension
  - With my manager/business owner background
    - Workflow and information value

How this webinar works

- You are muted
  - If you've been talking, hoping we'd notice, we can't hear you
- We're recording this webinar
  - None of your information appears in the final webinar
  - The recording link is provided to you automatically in a follow up email tomorrow
  - A short survey is also included
    - Helps us make the webinars better for you
- We should be done by the top of the hour
  - We know you have a busy day

Example agreement with guest speakers

I use the following content as my agreement with my guest speakers. Feel free to use what's useful to you but don't forget to run your version past your attorney.

Welcome to the *[insert company here]* Free Webinar Series

Thank you for your interest in presenting for the *[insert company here]* Free Webinar Series! We're excited to have you.

This document explains what we're doing, what the expectations are, the time frame of tasks, and the slide material we'd like to have inserted in your slides.

What is *[insert company here]* doing?

[insert company here] is doing a series of hour long free webinars on *[insert topics here]*. *[insert company here]* is trying to educate the *[insert community here]*. We know training budgets are insufficient and there are a lot of people who may not have kept their skills up to date.

We're offering topics that are generally tool-neutral.

What do we mean by tools-neutral?

Because these are not about *[insert company here]* products but may be about something that can be done in a product, you may talk about using other tools. If the thing can be done in our tools, we appreciate being included. If our tool is relevant, we prefer a fast reference and then refer the audience to our website for more details.

These webinars are NOT a cleverly disguised sales pitch on a topic. We're trying to help the community that made us successful by providing training on *[insert industry here]* topics.

Who is attending?

We're advertising to the general *[insert industry group here]* world through lists, groups, social media, and our Tech Support emails. We are getting 100 – 450 signed up per webinar, internationally. They may or may not use *[insert company here]* tools.

We expect you to also advertise: your website, communities you belong to, your blog, Twitter, Facebook, press releases, or any other way you can think of to get the word out about your webinar.

Can I promote myself during the webinar?

We expect you to quickly introduce yourself at the start of the webinar, including your name and contact information. We have no issues with a short – short – pitch about you and the services you may offer at the end of the webinar.

We would like you to thank *[insert company here]* at the end for providing the hosting for this free webinar.

Does *[insert company here]* make money from these?

No. We incur the expense of the free webinars and charge no one for attending.

Will I get paid?

No. We can probably get you some free *[insert company here]* product or service, but that may vary.

Does *[insert company here]* record these webinars?

We are recording the webinars, with your permission, and making them available after the webinar is over. You can also use that link. This makes the webinars work for the time zones that are bad for the time zone we try to do these at. Many people sign up with the expectation they will only view/listen to the recording.

Who owns the copyright?

[insert company here] wishes to make the recording available later but have no interest in any claims to the copyright for your slides or material. We do want to have the recording available, as above.

What equipment do I need?

You are completely responsible for gathering the equipment you need for your part of the webinar.

- A computer on a high speed connection to the Internet
- Slides of some sort for people to see
- Perhaps other applications with files, as needed for your topic
- Because these are webinars, you also need one of the following:
- Call into a toll number for the voice. *[insert company here]* will not reimburse you for the phone call.
- Use a microphone/headset connected to your computer to speak into so the VoIP and phone people can hear you. A Webcam with a microphone will not work. A stand alone microphone is not the best solution if you have your sound on to hear me or yourself, as the microphone will pick up the sound from your speakers. Logitech makes good quality microphone/headsets at about $30 US.

Is *[insert company here]* reviewing my slides for suitability?

We want your slides to review about a week ahead of your scheduled webinar. We are not reviewing to "approve" your content; we are making sure that we understand what you're saying so that we can intelligently answer the questions as they come in during the live webinar. We may have questions to make sure we understand where we're going.

We also have a sense of what people are asking about on the topics we're doing for the webinar so we may have input based on what people have asked in other webinars. We are not trying to control your message; we're trying to assure a high standard of quality.

Do I have to use the *[insert company here]* slide design?

Nope, an attractive and easy-to-read design is all we ask.

What if people have questions during the webinar?

A *[insert company here]* person, such as Sharon Burton, will answer the live questions in the Questions window while you give your topic. It is not possible to answer for you to the questions from 250 people live and give your topic at the same time.

If someone asks questions that the *[insert company here]* person cannot answer, they are typically told to follow up with the speaker offline.

Schedule of tasks

Your task	When	Notes
Send webinar write up to Name@*[insert company here]*.com, including your bio	6 to 8 weeks before the scheduled date	Review and save the meeting emails you get. One contains your login info for the webinar. Another is info you need to advertise your webinar.
Start publicizing the webinar	4 weeks before the scheduled date	Your blog, your sig line in email, an email to your customers, local industry communities, anywhere else you think might be interested.
Test the GoToWebinar and your equipment with Sharon Burton	2 weeks before the scheduled date	Sharon will log in and start the webinar. We should spend about 30 minutes making sure your equipment works and you understand the interface.

Your task	When	Notes
Send Sharon your slides	1 week before the scheduled date	Sharon will review and ask any questions or for clarification.
Login to the webinar software, using your login info emailed to you 6 to 8 weeks prior	30 minutes before the scheduled start time	Sharon will work with you to make sure you know what to do when you start. Sharon will start the recording when you're ready to start, but at least ten minutes before the scheduled hour.
Finish the webinar and thank people for attending	1 hour after the scheduled start time	We want the webinars to be what we said they would – 1 hour. Sharon stops recording. There may be a live question and answer period if you have time.
When people are logged off, close the webinar down	About 1 hour and 10 minutes	Hand the controls back to Sharon and she will stop the webinar.
The recorded webinar will be available	About 4 hours after the webinar is over	Sharon will render the recording and upload it.

Requested slide content

We have been doing these webinars for a while and would like the following information on slides in your presentation

After you introduce yourself, we'd like the following content on 2 slides. Feel free to edit:

> We also have with us…
>
> Sharon Burton
>
> - *[insert company here] [insert job title or role here]*
>
> She will answer your questions during the presentation
>
> - She'll do her best to answer them
> - Type questions in the Question area of the webinar bar

> How this webinar works
>
> - You are muted
>   - If you've been talking, hoping we'd notice, we can't hear you
> - We're recording this webinar
> - None of your information will appear in the final webinar
> - The recording link will be provided to you automatically in a follow up email
> - A short survey will also be included
> - We should be done by the top of the hour
> - We know you have a busy day

At the end, we'd like the following content on 1 slide.

Thanks!

- Thank you to *[insert company here]* Software for organizing this webinar.
- Thank you to participants for attending.

Index

A

Adobe Connect, 29
advertising, 2, 31
agreement
    sample, 75-78
    webinar, 24
animations, 46
announcing, 36
    schedule for, 42
Anymeeting, 29
attendance
    avoiding low, 69
    setting expectations, 54
audience, 15-16
audio, 27

B

backup person, 50-51
    importance of, 71
backup plans, 49
bait-and-switch, 70
blogs
    promoting on, 37
    responding to negative posts, 66
    timing posts, 42

C

Click Webinar, 29
clips, posting, 64
computer
    preparing, 56
    requirements, 25
cost
    per-attendee, 1
    webinar services, 29
CRM (Customer Relationship Management), 64
Customer Relationship Management (CRM), 64
customer support
    as webinar leader, 9

D

discussion lists, 40

E

educational webinars, 7, 20
email
    follow up, 65, 67
    promotional, 37
equipment requirements, 25
evaluation, 66

F

Facebook, 38
features, webinar service, 30
follow up, 63-67
    email, 65, 67
    importance of, 72

G

giveaways, 48
Google+, 38
GoToMeeting, 29
GoToWebinar, 29
guest speakers, 23, 41
    customers as, 24
    sample agreement, 75-78

H

hash tag, twitter, 38, 46
headset, importance of, 26

I

introductions, 60

L

leader, selecting, 8-11
leads
    following up, 65
    generating, 64
LinkedIn, 40
LiveMeeting, 29
logistics, 50

M

management
    as webinar leader, 10

time required, 12-13
marketing speak, 32
marketing team
    as webinar leader, 8
mistakes, 11, 17, 69-72
mobile devices, 28
multiple presenters, 49
muting, 59
    importance of, 71

N

news groups, 40

O

outages, handling, 49

P

planning, 36
    importance of, 6, 44
polls, 47
posting schedule
    sample, 42
preparation, 43-51
    importance of, 44
    slides, 44
presentation
    preparing, 44
    slides, 73-74
presenters
    multiple, 49
    preparing, 58
press release, 41
pricing, webinar service, 29
product-specific webinars, 21
promotion, 37-42

Q
questions, 47, 61

R
ReadyTalk, 29
recording
    agreement, 24
    disclosure, 60
    importance of, 72
    posting, 63
    starting, 60
    web page, 37
relationships
    building customer, 16
    follow up, 65
reminders, 54
    schedule for, 42
resources
    equipment, 25
    estimating time required, 12

S
sales team
    as webinar leader, 8
    coordinating with, 67
sample write-up, 34
schedule
    importance of maintaining, 70
    posting, 36, 42
scheduling
    30 minutes before, 57
    after it's over, 63
    frequency, 21
    geographical considerations, 22
    picking the day of the week, 22
    picking the time of day, 21
    picking the time of year, 18

    three hours before, 55
    week before, 53
series
    expanding, 18
    initial topics, 17
    planning, 16
sign up guidelines, 35
signups, monitoring, 53
slides
    animations, 46
    introductory, 45
    preparing, 44
    samples, 73-74
social media, 38-42
    tracking responses, 65
sound check, 59
starting time, 59
survey
    post-webinar, 65

T
tablets, presenting with, 27
technology
    mistakes, 70
    testing, 54
technology requirements, 25
tools-neutral webinars, 19
topics
    adding, 18
    choosing, 15
    planning initial, 17
    scheduling, 21
training team
    as webinar leader, 9
twitter, 38
    hash tags, 38, 46

V

virtual machines, 56
VoIP, 26

W

web site
    posting recordings on, 63
webcams, 27, 57
WebEx, 29
webinar services
    evaluating, 29
    table, 29
webinars
    definition, 1
    educational, 7
    reasons to run, 5
    who should run?, 8-11
website
    announcing on your, 36
white paper
    importance of, 72
white papers, 48
write-up
    sample, 34

Y

YouTube, 64

About the author

Sharon Burton is a nationally recognized expert, public speaker, and instructor in the field of business and technical communication. With 20 years of experience in the field, she has consulted with companies large and small, such as Pitney Bowes, Royal, and Hewlett Packard, to improve their product documentation and documentation workflow. Most recently, she is using her experience to help companies develop excellent webinars.

Sharon has received numerous honors for her work, including the distinction of Associate Fellow by the Society for Technical Communication. She was recently identified as the 18th most influential person in the world on the topics of technical communication and content strategy by Mindtouch, Inc.

Sharon is a PhD candidate in Cultural Anthropology and an adjunct professor at the University of California, Riverside, teaching technical communications to engineering majors and post-graduates. A sometimes newspaper columnist and essayist, her articles on life in Southern California have appeared in such periodicals as the Los Angeles Times, the Inland Empire Weekly and the Inland Valley Voice newspapers.

She can be reached at sharon@sharonburton.com.

About XML Press

XML Press (http://xmlpress.net) was founded in 2008 to publish content that helps technical communicators be more effective. Our publications support managers, social media practitioners, technical communicators, content strategists, and the engineers who support their efforts.

Our publications are available through most retailers, and discounted pricing is available for volume purchases for business, educational, or promotional use.

For more information, send email to orders@xmlpress.net or call us at (970) 231-3624.